Increasing Confidence

Philippa Davies

LONDON, NEW YORK, MUNICH,
MELBOURNE, DELHI

Project Editor Nicky Munro
Senior Art Editor Sarah Cowley
DTP Designer Rajen Shah
Production Controller Mandy Inness

Managing Editor Adèle Hayward
Managing Art Editor Marianne Markham
Category Publisher Stephanie Jackson

Produced for Dorling Kindersley by

Cooling Brown
9–11 High Street, Hampton
Middlesex TW12 2SA

Creative Director Arthur Brown
Managing Editor Amanda Lebentz
Designers Elaine Hewson, Elly King, Tish Jones

First published in Great Britain in 2003
by Dorling Kindersley Limited, 80 Strand
London WC2R 0RL

A Penguin Company

2 4 6 8 10 9 7 5 3 1

Copyright © 2003 Dorling Kindersley Limited
Text copyright © 2003 Philippa Davies

All rights reserved. No part of this publication
may be reproduced, stored in a retrieval
system, or transmitted in any form or by any
means, electronic, mechanical, photocopying,
recording, or otherwise, without prior
permission of the copyright owner.

A CIP catalogue record for this book is available
from the British Library
ISBN 0 7513 4894 5

Reproduced by Colourscan, Singapore
Printed in Hong Kong by Wing King Tong

See our complete catalogue at
www.dk.com

Contents

Introduction

Confidence is a very precious commodity. Those who possess it find it easier to learn new skills, to make friends, to enjoy happy relationships, to adapt to change, and to achieve what they want in life. With confidence, life is simply far more enjoyable. Increasing Confidence is a practical guide to taking charge of your life and making positive changes. It helps you assess your current level of confidence, identify areas for improvement, motivate yourself, and plan your confidence-building programme. You will learn how to project a more confident image as well as build deep-down lasting confidence to ensure that you fulfil your potential in life. Packed with tips, exercises, inspirational quotations, and morale-boosting affirmations, this inspiring book will help you feel that you can take on the world – whatever the situation!

Understanding Confidence

Confidence affects a person's capacity to enjoy life's ups and cope with its downs. It is a very personal feeling, so to build confidence you need to know what triggers it in you.

Defining Confidence

Confidence is often associated with feeling happy, energetic, lighthearted, and generally in control of life. Explore what confidence means to you and you will have a clearer understanding of what you need to do in order to increase it.

WHAT IS CONFIDENCE?

Most people regard being confident as having faith in their own abilities, a sense of purpose in life, and the belief that, within reason, they will be able to do what they wish, plan, and expect. Self-confident people have realistic expectations, and are able to accept themselves and remain positive even when some of those expectations are not met. Most people feel more confident in certain areas of life than in others. For example, you might see yourself as talented in a particular sport, or skilled professionally, while being less sure of yourself in social situations.

▲ **Having confidence**
Confidence gives you courage to tackle challenges because it makes you aware that learning from an experience is far more important than success or failure.

BEING CONFIDENT

Whether taking a driving test or meeting the chief executive, being confident is a major asset in life. It helps you deal with uncertainty, see challenges as opportunities, take calculated risks, and make swift decisions. Confidence is also important when you want to participate in public life, such as when joining a society. At work, confidence improves your effectiveness in interviews, meetings, and presentations, and in dealing with clients and colleagues.

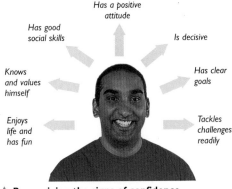

Has a positive attitude

Has good social skills

Is decisive

Knows and values himself

Has clear goals

Enjoys life and has fun

Tackles challenges readily

▲ **Recognizing the signs of confidence**
Confident people have a go-getting attitude, are more willing to take risks, and enjoy new experiences. They are comfortable with themselves and tend to be relaxed in social situations.

FOCUS POINT

● Think back to the last time that you felt really good about yourself – what was the occasion?

DEFINING CONFIDENCE FOR YOURSELF

To define what confidence means to you, think of a situation in which you felt supremely confident and try to describe your feelings. You might say, for example, "I felt valued", "I felt in control", "I felt that my achievement had been recognized", or "I felt that I was being listened to and taken seriously". By analyzing what makes you feel good about yourself, you can aim to incorporate more morale-boosting experiences into your life, and so keep your self-esteem high.

New author is aware of confidence boost at seeing her words in print

Friend praises aspiring author for having her article published

◀ **Sensing accomplishment**
Try to identify what makes you feel really proud of yourself. Do you feel good when receiving praise, solving a problem, or creating something, for example?

Benefiting from Confidence

*L*ife is simply better when lived with *confidence. Recognize the benefits that confidence can bring, from increasing your opportunities to improving relationships, and you will see how much you can gain by addressing any confidence gaps you have.*

FOCUS POINT

● Build your confidence and you will expand your capacity for happiness and fulfilment.

Fact File

Pyschologists have identified what is termed "self-efficacy", that is, how confident a person feels about their effectiveness. It has been found that self-efficacy levels influence motivation and how well people tackle a task. It has also been shown that people with high self-efficacy feel more positive about life in general.

ATTRACTING OPPORTUNITIES

When you are confident, others are likely to want to entrust you with new challenges, difficult problems to solve, and tasks that require strong leadership. You will also attract more opportunities in everyday life; for example, you are more likely to be asked to help organize community or school projects, or to get involved in other activities. Another benefit of confidence is that it makes you more attractive to other people – a lack of defensiveness and a desire for engagement with others is a powerful magnet. For this reason, confident people tend to receive more invitations to attend parties and other social events.

Approaches neighbours for help with community gardening project

◀ **Winning support**
Confident people project enthusiasm, which in turn enthuses others. It is invaluable when you are trying to convince or win support from people.

Impressed by her friendly, confident attitude, couple agree to help

66Wishing to be friends is quick work, but friendship is a slow ripening fruit.**99**

Aristotle

FORGING RELATIONSHIPS

Just as confidence helps people to initiate friendships, it also helps to build positive, mutually beneficial relationships over the long term. Rather than envy what others have or look to others to supply what you may lack, confidence gives you a clear sense of the boundaries between yourself and others. With confidence, it is also easier to accept rejection as a one-off event, rather than allowing it to erode your core self-belief. When difficulties arise, having confidence means that you are more likely to have faith in your ability to work through problems by staying in the relationship. If a relationship does finally break down, you are also less likely to feel threatened by the prospect of being alone.

◀ **Pursuing your own interests**
Confidence improves relationships because friends and partners trust each other, which means giving one another the freedom to play a favourite sport or enjoy pastimes that are not necessarily shared.

FEELING IN CONTROL

When you feel confident, you believe that you are more self-determining, that you can take the initiative, influence others, and make things happen. People experience greatest stress when they feel they have little control over what is happening in their lives. When this happens, self-belief is low, and the damaging effects of stress are likely to be felt more profoundly. If you are able to do something about a situation, you are far less likely to succumb to stress. Even when life gets on top of you and you feel overwhelmed, you are far more likely to believe that you can recover quickly afterwards.

At a Glance

- The more confident you are, the more capable you appear to others, and so you attract more opportunities.

- Confidence helps you form nourishing relationships that are mutually beneficial.

- The greater your confidence levels, the better equipped you are to deal with life's adversities and the more resilient you are.

COPING WITH CRISES

When you are confident that you can solve problems and rise to challenges, you are able to cope with crises more easily. You are more likely to respond to difficult situations by saying to yourself, "There must be a way around this", "Who can help me with this?", or "I've weathered storms like this before, I can weather this one." Confidence helps you deal with failure, too. Rather than thinking, "I'm useless", the attitude of a confident person is, "I didn't get it right that time – how can I do it differently next time?" Failure is seen as a one-off event rather than an indication of deeper or more permanent inadequacy.

FOCUS POINT

● Use the knowledge you gain from an upsetting experience to help you cope with future difficulties.

Recommends specialist to help with problem

Overcoming a Crisis

See the crisis as a challenge that requires purposeful action

⬇

Look at the facts of the crisis – you need to know what you are dealing with

⬇

Focus on a positive outcome and plan the steps you need to take to achieve it

⬇

Get help from family, friends, or an objective outsider

▲ **Supporting others in a crisis**
Confidence in your ability to overcome problems makes you better able to support other people in times of turmoil. Your own experience can also prove invaluable when someone needs advice.

Useful Exercises

▶ Think back to the most recent crisis you experienced and remember the strengths you drew on at the time to bolster your confidence.

▶ If you have a tendency to become flustered during a crisis, stop yourself and ask, "What is it absolutely vital that I do here?"

▶ Relearn some childlike ways of venting anger or frustration, such as stamping your feet or hitting a cushion, to help diffuse tension.

LEARNING THROUGHOUT LIFE

Being confident makes you more open to learning and experimenting in life, leading to greater self-fulfilment and emotional growth. Confidence has nothing to do with being self-satisfied or superior. It means being happy to admit that you have failings, that you do not know everything, and have plenty to learn. Confident people have fewer problems with role changes because they see change as an opportunity for learning, and so will throw themselves into a new job, life in a new area, or retirement. With confidence, you also learn more because you are more attentive to what is happening around you. This is because you are not overly concerned by what others think of you, or preoccupied with maintaining a defensive front to cover up your insecurities.

▲ **Adapting to parenthood**
Confidence makes it easier to adapt to new roles, such as becoming a parent. This is because confident people believe that they have the resources to cope with life's major challenges.

Case Study

NAME: Sandy

ISSUE: Feels unfulfilled in her life

OBJECTIVE: To learn new skills, build confidence

Sandy, a divorced mother, has brought up her five-year-old son alone, with some support from her family. Now that he is at school, she would like to do something more with her life. When she hears that her son's school is looking for parents to provide reading support in the classroom, she volunteers. Although nervous at first, Sandy is surprised at how much she enjoys helping the children, and at how effective she is. Encouraged by the class teacher, Sandy researches teacher training courses and is accepted on a programme. This boosts her confidence to apply for a part-time job, and she is offered the position. On her teaching course, she meets someone with whom she starts a relationship. By the time her son is 10, she has a good job in a local school, and derives enormous confidence from having turned her life around.

Living Without Confidence

There are many drawbacks to lacking confidence, not least of which is that you are not getting the most out of life. Understand how living without confidence can lead to missed opportunities, damaged relationships, and vulnerability to stress.

PLAYING IT SAFE

Without the confidence to handle problems, the tendency is to avoid risks and challenges of all descriptions: from giving a speech at a friend's wedding to asking the boss for a pay rise, to going on a training course to learn a new skill. Other people may start to view you as timid and fearful and avoid offering you opportunities. Why should they have confidence in your ability to tackle something if you clearly do not have it yourself? When people view you in this way, they become more protective and you may start to get used to this attentiveness and begin relating to them in a childlike way. This can make it extremely difficult for them to view you as a responsible adult.

Self-Talk

Repeat the following positive messages to yourself to help build your self-belief.

> **"**I'm much tougher than people might think.**"**

> **"**I'm quite capable of handling this situation.**"**

> **"**It is not what happens to me but how I handle it that determines my emotional wellbeing.**"**

▼ **Taking control**
People who lack confidence may be passive and allow others to take control. To build confidence you need to take responsibility and take action yourself.

Friend offers to take charge and organize social event

Declines offer firmly

FOCUS POINT

● Develop a positive "have-a-go" attitude – instead of saying "Why?" try to get into the habit of saying "Why not?"

12

SPOILING RELATIONSHIPS

A lack of confidence can damage relationships because people with little confidence feel envious and resentful of their confident friends, family, colleagues, or partners. Making harsh comparisons is unrealistic and leads to disappointment. Instead of resenting confident people, realize what you can learn from them. What do they do to convey confidence? Can you behave in a similar way?

Shows photos of her recent parachute jump

Admits fear of heights and praises friend's courage

Enjoying good relationships ▶
You and your friends all have unique life stories, skills, and talents, so appreciate your differences rather than think you are lacking.

FOCUS POINTS

● Accept that your confidence may be knocked sometimes, but don't let this damage your positive self-esteem.

● Avoid putting yourself down – everyone lacks confidence sometimes.

SUCCUMBING TO STRESS

Low self-esteem and frequent feelings of timidity lower resistance in the immune system, increasing both physical and psychological vulnerability to the effects of stress. Without confidence, you may view change with trepidation because you feel you lack the resources to cope. You may even start to behave in a way that ensures a negative outcome, like the person who predicts they will fail an exam and then leaves revision until the last moment, so that at least they feel that they have been right about something.

Things to Do	Things to Avoid
✓ Do remember that you are a fallible human being and that even super-confident people make mistakes.	✗ Avoid blaming others for your lack of confidence – whatever has happened in the past, you are responsible for yourself.
✓ Do think about what you have managed to do rather than what you believe you should have been doing.	✗ Avoid feeling sorry for yourself or acting like a "victim" and look at how to change your behaviour.
✓ Do learn to appreciate your good points.	✗ Avoid focusing on your bad points.

Understanding How We Acquire Confidence

While it is possible that confidence is influenced by genes, there is no evidence to support the theory. Your level of confidence is affected by your wellbeing, your past experiences, how you see yourself, and how you perceive that others see you.

FOCUS POINT

● Although confidence can be nurtured by others, it will diminish unless you nurture it yourself.

Fact File

There is evidence to suggest that eldest children, only children, and children with only one sibling generally achieve more in life, which points to higher confidence levels. This is probably because such children tend to receive more parental attention. Eldest children often identify strongly with their parents and are more conformist and conservative than their younger siblings.

LEARNING FROM FAMILY

As children, much of what we make of the world, our place in it, and the route our lives are likely to take is learned from our parents or significant carers. Some people are lucky enough to have had parents who understood the value of confidence-building. Others, whose parents themselves may have been struggling, may have received little help. However, research shows that children from very disadvantaged backgrounds can fare well in life if one significant adult – not necessarily a parent – helps to build their confidence. There are many prominent figures who have developed great confidence under the influence of an aunt, teacher, grandparent, or concerned friend.

Father encourages daughter to brush teeth properly

Building self-esteem ▶
Children imitate their parents, so they are far more likely to look after themselves and learn to be independent and self-nurturing in later life if their parents lead by example.

Useful Exercises

▶ Think of a recent experience that greatly boosted your confidence, remember how it made you feel, and store the memory for the future.

▶ Use bolstering self-talk when faced with difficulties, reminding yourself how you have successfully handled such situations in the past.

▶ Give yourself some time at the end of each day to ruminate on events and congratulate yourself on aspects that you think you have handled well.

LEARNING FROM EXPERIENCE

We develop confidence through varied and challenging experiences in life – particularly those that we feel we have tackled well. In order to learn the most from experience, you need to put or find yourself in situations in which you do not have all the answers, and so risk losing face. It is important to admit that you "don't know". When you then take what you believe to be the right course of action and other people confirm that your judgement was sound, the boost to your confidence is considerable. The more such experiences you have, the more confident you will become.

66Experience is the best teacher.**99**

Proverb

LEARNING FROM FAILURE

Failure – painful though it may be – can in fact build lasting confidence. By finding out what went wrong, and what could be done differently next time, you can turn every failure into a learning opportunity. No one tastes true success by living a very safe, uneventful existence; failure must be experienced along the way. What is important is the way in which you handle failure. If a parent or teacher made you feel inadequate as a child simply because you did something in an inadequate way, you may have developed an acute sensitivity towards failure. This can lead you to shun new experiences in order to preserve your confidence. Avoid taking failure personally, and see it as a chance to improve.

Resolves to work on her interview technique for next time

Handling rejection ▶
Develop a philosophical attitude to rejection. An unsuccessful job application may represent failure, but it is an opportunity to build confidence by learning from your mistakes.

Analyzing How We Lose Confidence

Knowing what has knocked your confidence in the past can make you less vulnerable to such influences in the future. Analyze the reasons behind your insecurities and move from an emotional response to a more reasoned one.

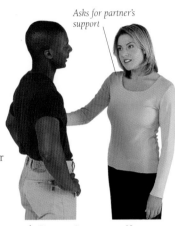

Asks for partner's support

LACKING ENCOURAGEMENT
Parents, teachers, work colleagues, and family members who are heavily preoccupied with their own lives may have little time or energy left to encourage others. As children, our natural propensity to feel good about ourselves can be severely diminished by a lack of attention. As adults, feeling taken for granted, ignored, or rejected, especially by someone whom we like, love, or respect can seriously damage our self-esteem, particularly if the behaviour continues for a prolonged period of time.

▲ **Preserving your self-esteem**
If someone close to you is unsupportive and causing you to lose confidence, let them know how you are feeling. Explain how important their encouragement is and how much you value their input.

FOCUS POINTS

● When times are hard take comfort from the fact that situations change – usually for the better.

● Accept that spells of bad luck are part of the normal pattern of living and not a reflection on you.

EXPERIENCING BAD LUCK
The occasional incidence of bad luck happens to everyone and is usually soon forgotten. However, continued or serious misfortune can be very damaging to confidence. For example, falling ill and then encountering a major life change can cause someone to lose confidence in their ability to cope. An exhausted new parent who also has to deal with demanding changes at work may find that their confidence plummets. In such circumstances, a firm set of values and beliefs can help you weather misfortune and maintain confidence levels.

CHOOSING THE WRONG GOALS

Pursuing goals that do not support our values can erode confidence. Working solely for financial gain, for example, when you would prefer to help others or make better use of your skills may be demoralizing. Since self-respect is fundamental to self-confidence, you are unlikely to feel good about yourself unless you are also living a life that reflects your own values. To clarify your values, identify those achievements that mean the most to you – has creating a happy family life meant more than career success, for example?

BEING CRITICIZED

Criticism can undermine confidence when it makes people feel that they are in some way inadequate or are being unfairly targeted. Being "put down" or criticized – especially in situations where it is difficult to defend yourself – can be particularly humiliating. Keep in mind that although you may not like being criticized, or agree with what is being said, you can still learn from the thoughts and views of others.

Listens as manager gives reasons for criticism

Handling criticism positively ▶
Ask for clarification of the criticism, if necessary, and avoid responding until you have assessed whether or not the criticism is valid.

Things to Do

✓ Do seek out and spend more time with people who actively encourage you in your goals.

✓ Do be selective about the goals you set yourself and make sure that they reflect your values.

✓ Do ask for examples of what someone means if their criticisms are unclear.

Things to Avoid

✗ Avoid spending time with people who discourage you.

✗ Avoid setting over-ambitious goals and trying to be perfect at everything you do.

✗ Avoid reacting emotionally to criticism, particularly when someone is attacking your character.

Is Lack of Confidence Holding You Back?

Evaluate whether or not you would benefit from building confidence by responding to the following statements. Mark the answers that are closest to your experience. If your answer is "Never", mark Option 1; if it is "Always", mark Option 4; and so on. Add your scores together, and refer to the analysis for guidance.

Options	
1	Never
2	Occasionally
3	Frequently
4	Always

How Do You Respond?

	1	2	3	4
1 I have a poor opinion of myself.	☐	☐	☐	☐
2 I generally feel tired and lacking in energy.	☐	☐	☐	☐
3 I dread the start of each working day.	☐	☐	☐	☐
4 My concentration is generally poor.	☐	☐	☐	☐
5 I find it difficult to say "no" to people.	☐	☐	☐	☐
6 I am reluctant to voice my opinions.	☐	☐	☐	☐
7 I wish life was different.	☐	☐	☐	☐
8 I tend to avoid people whom I find difficult.	☐	☐	☐	☐
9 I avoid difficult situations.	☐	☐	☐	☐

	1	2	3	4
10 I postpone making decisions.	☐	☐	☐	☐
11 If I cannot decide, I leave it to fate.	☐	☐	☐	☐
12 I feel nervous for no apparent reason.	☐	☐	☐	☐
13 I feel self-conscious about my appearance.	☐	☐	☐	☐
14 I was lonely as a child.	☐	☐	☐	☐
15 I was bullied as a child.	☐	☐	☐	☐
16 My teachers were unkind to me.	☐	☐	☐	☐
17 My family found fault with me as a child.	☐	☐	☐	☐
18 I find it difficult to talk to strangers.	☐	☐	☐	☐

	1	2	3	4
19 I feel that life is passing me by.	☐	☐	☐	☐
20 My relationships are strained.	☐	☐	☐	☐
21 I consider others' feelings before mine.	☐	☐	☐	☐
22 I dread speaking in public.	☐	☐	☐	☐
23 I shy away from responsibility.	☐	☐	☐	☐
24 I worry about the future.	☐	☐	☐	☐
25 I focus on my failures not my successes.	☐	☐	☐	☐

	1	2	3	4
26 I feel negative towards people around me.	☐	☐	☐	☐
27 I worry what other people think of me.	☐	☐	☐	☐
28 I can be brash and aggressive.	☐	☐	☐	☐
29 I feel inferior to other people.	☐	☐	☐	☐
30 I wish that life was more fun.	☐	☐	☐	☐
31 I feel dreadful if I make a mistake.	☐	☐	☐	☐
32 I respond badly to criticism.	☐	☐	☐	☐

Analysis

When you have added up your scores, look at the analysis below to establish whether a lack of confidence is holding you back. Make a note of your weakest and strongest points to help you plan your confidence-building strategy.

32–64 You are confident in most situations. However, you may still need to develop confidence in certain areas.

65–95 You have reasonable self-esteem, but need to work on some situations that make you feel self-conscious.

96–128 Your self-esteem is low and you would gain considerable benefits from increasing your confidence and starting to fulfil your potential in life.

My weakest points are:

_____
_____
_____
_____

My strongest points are:

_____
_____
_____
_____

Preparing to Build Your Confidence

A successful confidence-building campaign requires an organized approach. Gather your resolve, set specific goals, seek support, and put the past behind you to get off to a good start.

Motivating Yourself

Confidence-building requires a high level of self-motivation. Make a commitment to change and to overcome fears that have held you back, visualize success, and develop the positive frame of mind you need in order to rise to the challenges ahead.

FOCUS POINT

● Imagine a situation where more confidence would make a big difference to how you feel about yourself.

At a Glance

● Confidence cannot be achieved overnight – it requires time and commitment.

● It is important to take responsibility for your own choices in life rather than blame others when things go wrong.

● Overcoming your fears becomes easier once you know exactly what it is that you are afraid of.

MAKING A COMMITMENT

When life is going well, people tend to attribute their success to themselves. When life is going badly, people often attribute their failures to others, or to external circumstances. While it may be tempting to blame others, or your situation, for your lack of confidence, you must tackle confidence-building yourself. The best time to start addressing the issue is now – because if you wait until circumstances are perfect, you will never get started. Excuses such as "The time's not right", or "I've got too much on just now", mean that you are simply avoiding the issue.

OVERCOMING FEAR

Fear of failure causes people to avoid situations in which they risk feeling humiliated and losing face in front of others. However, it is through failure that you learn the most, and the most successful people are those who have experienced numerous failures. Avoid being too negatively self-critical and imagining that others are more interested in your performance than they actually are. The first step in reducing fear is to admit that you are scared. Fearful people are defensive – they may deny that they are scared, or refuse to accept that they have a problem. By acknowledging your fears, and taking steps to overcome them, you enlarge your world and develop more choices, and life becomes easier as your confidence grows.

Useful Exercises

▶ Tackle fear in everyday situations, such as by chatting to people while waiting for the bus, or volunteering to make a speech at your hobby group.

▶ Acknowledge and make light of your fears in front of others, for example by saying, "I'm much too nervous to do this – but no one else would!"

Feels scared because she will not know many of the people attending

Accepts invitation and determines to enjoy the event

Friend calls with an invitation to social event

Replies that she is busy and unable to attend party

Makes excuse of checking diary to allow time to think

▲ Dealing with fear

This scenario illustrates two different ways of responding to a daunting invitation – one is to react with fear and issue an immediate refusal, while the other is to allow a moment to acknowledge the fear, refuse to be ruled by it, and take the opportunity to overcome it.

Faces weekend alone and misses chance to overcome fear

Recognizing How Fear Can Affect Performance

Type of Fear	Effect
Conflict	Passive behaviour, unable to stand up for oneself, reluctant to express opinion or to risk being rejected.
Appearing incompetent	Defensive behaviour, avoids probing questions, over-emphasis on detail, unable to answer questions with "I don't know".
Being seen as insignificant	Aggressive behaviour, may express extreme opinions to seek attention, shows lack of concern for others.
Losing control	Aggressive behaviour, tendency to control situations, dislikes unpredictability, ignores others' opinions.

FOCUS POINT

● Keep a vision of the "new confident you" in mind as you work towards making it a reality.

VISUALIZING SUCCESS

An excellent motivator is to envisage the gains to be made from tackling your fears and increasing your confidence. Rather than look back and regret what you might have achieved if you had been more confident, imagine what you will be capable of doing or being when you have confidence. Instead of focusing on the difficulties ahead, concentrate on your potential. Think of situations in which you have lacked confidence in the past and visualize yourself handling them successfully. See yourself as you would like to be – smiling, happy, relaxed, or being assertive at work, for example. Make your image vivid, clear, and vibrant.

Manager is impressed by employee's calm, direct approach

Employee recognizes boss's budget concerns, and gives clear reasons for pay rise

◀ Keeping a perspective
When you feel scared of a situation, such as asking the boss for a pay rise, focus on the other person's position. Thinking about what the other party hopes to gain helps you to think and act empathetically.

UNDERSTANDING MOODS

There are four distinct moods – energetic but calm, energetic and tense, tired and calm, and tired and tense. Ideally, you should aim to tackle your confidence-building activities when you are in the best frame of mind, which is when you are feeling energetic and calm. For many people this is during mid-morning, while mid-afternoon is the most common time to experience a slump.

Plotting your moods
Keep a note of your mood changes in a journal over several days to help you identify when you usually feel at your best.

CREATING A GOOD MOOD

It is easier to motivate yourself when you are in a good mood. Because moods are influenced by associations, you can lift your mood simply by reminding yourself of something pleasant and uplifting. Consider what you really enjoy doing and find utterly absorbing. It could be gardening, playing with the children, home improvement, painting, or cooking. Sit quietly for five minutes and imagine yourself performing this activity. This will improve your mood and help you maintain a sense of perspective about what matters in life. It is also useful preparation for any confidence-building challenge, such as making a speech or tackling someone about a difficult issue.

▲ **Boosting mood with exercise**
Exercise is known to improve mood because it releases endorphins, known as "feel-good" hormones, into the bloodstream.

Things to Do	Things to Avoid
✓ Do exercise regularly to help keep you in a positive frame of mind.	✗ Avoid short-term boosts like coffee, alcohol, drugs, cigarettes, and sugar.
✓ Do try an energizing form of exercise, such as aerobics, brisk walking, or swimming, if you feel tired and tense.	✗ Avoid struggling on doggedly when you are tired and tense. Give yourself a break, even if only for 10 minutes.
✓ Do choose a calming form of exercise, such as Pilates or yoga, if you feel energetic and tense.	✗ Avoid leaving everything until the last minute or you will regularly find yourself in a fraught mood.

Setting Your Confidence Goals

Goal-setting involves creating a clear idea of what you want to achieve, and analyzing how you will know when you have achieved it. Choose goals that reflect your own priorities and make them specific so that you know exactly what to aim for.

FOCUS POINT

● Set time aside to plan your confidence-building goal and visualize the progress you wish to make.

Considering Your Goals

Think about what you want to achieve

⬇

Make sure that whatever you aim for reflects your personal values

⬇

Check that your goals are challenging yet realistic

⬇

Assess whether you will need help or resources to achieve your goals

⬇

Decide how to measure progress and define success

WHY SET GOALS?

Goals are motivational not only because they give you targets to aim for but also because they represent what is important to you. So, for example, setting a goal of speaking well in public is likely to mean that you are enthusiastic about your subject and want to be able to do it justice. Or, if your goal is to socialize with people at parties, it may be that building relationships through overcoming shyness is important to you. Make your goals moderately difficult. If they are too stretching, you risk disappointment; if they are too easy, you are likely to lose interest. Consider how you will measure your progress and define success. For example, if your goal is to socialize with people at parties, will you have reached it after socializing at one party, or will success involve meeting new people at several parties?

❝Nothing great was ever achieved without enthusiasm.❞

Franklin D. Roosevelt

CHOOSING THE RIGHT GOALS

Your goals must support and reflect your own values if you are to achieve them. You are unlikely to be motivated by a goal that reflects someone else's priorities, or one that simply fails to inspire you. Avoid setting too many goals in different areas of your life because this will make you feel overstretched and unfocused. Ideally, you should start off with three clear goals, for example one personal, one professional, and one to do with health and fitness. Alternatively you could opt for three goals in one area that you really want to improve – such as your social life, career prospects, or relationships.

Keeping fit reflects concern for health

Being true to yourself ▶
If you feel that your confidence would be increased if you improved your fitness, start an exercise programme. If your goal is important to you, you are more likely to achieve it.

MAKING GOALS SPECIFIC

Goals need to be specific so that it is clear what you are striving for. So a goal such as "I want to be more confident with people" needs to be clarified to become "I want to start conversations with people at parties with confidence." Then you may want to progress to "I want to stand up for myself more at work", or "I want to speak with more confidence at my book club meetings."

Assessing Your Priorities

To help you assess what matters most to you in life, read the statements below and tick those with which you strongly agree.

- Being original and creative is important ☐
- I like to be efficient and avoid waste ☐
- I think it is important to care about others ☐
- I like to be effective and make things happen ☐
- I want to inspire and lead others well ☐
- I want to nurture and help others to grow ☐
- I am idealistic and want to help to change the world ☐
- I enjoy taking responsibility and managing projects ☐
- I am a team player and like to contribute to group effort ☐
- I need to achieve financial, emotional, or professional security ☐

Analysis Up to three ticks means that you know your priorities and should set your confidence goals accordingly. If you have ticked more than three boxes, you need to assess what is really important to you in order to set specific goals.

Planning Your Approach

Once you know what you want, it is important to have a practical plan that maps out how you are going to get there. Consider progressing towards your ultimate goal in stages, set time frames, and keep checking that your goals are appropriate.

Case Study

NAME: Francesca
ISSUE: Nervousness
OBJECTIVE: To speak at a conference

Francesca has a new role as a charity fundraiser and has been invited to speak at a business conference by its hosts, who support the charity. She is very nervous but, with advance warning, resolves to plan her approach. First, she volunteers to speak at several small local meetings. Then she takes charge at a larger fund-raising gathering. Meanwhile, she attends a public speaking training course. She takes every opportunity to chair meetings and when the conference arrives, while still a little nervous, Francesca feels satisfied with her performance.

PACING YOURSELF

Breaking down a general goal into components will make it easier to be clear about your progress. If your ultimate goal is to socialize with confidence and meet more people, you could start with a mini-goal of meeting one or two new people at the next social event you attend. Then you could build that up to three or four people and so on, until you build your confidence to the extent that you feel comfortable chatting to an entire roomful of people.

Seeks feedback on his delivery

▲ **Tackling a mini-goal**
If your goal is to speak in front of an audience, use mini-goals as stepping stones to success. Practise in front of a friend or family member first, then you might address a group of friends.

▲ Working out a timetable
Give yourself plenty of time in which to work towards your goal. Take your prior commitments into account and make sure that you allow for the unexpected.

SETTING TIME FRAMES

It is better to overestimate the time needed to achieve your goal than to give yourself too little time and set yourself up for disappointment. Remember to allow for unexpected setbacks, distractions, and shifting priorities along the way. Consider how much time you will realistically be able to set aside each week, or month, to devote to your confidence-building goals. You need to build in time to record your progress and feelings, to reflect on what you have learned, and for supplementary activities such as relaxation and meditation, that will help your self-development.

REVIEWING GOALS

It is important to check regularly that your goals remain appropriate. Circumstances change, and you could find that some of your goals become less important as a result. For example, if you decide to move home it may prove more useful to focus on a goal of building your confidence socially over the next few months so that you will be able to settle into your new location and get to know new friends more quickly.

FOCUS POINTS

● See yourself gradually overcoming your reticence as you pursue your goals.

● If a goal is proving to be too ambitious, change it to a more attainable one.

COMMITTING GOALS TO PAPER

Writing down goals can help you to achieve them because once you have committed them to paper they seem more concrete. Even more effective is to draw the outcome of the goals that you want to achieve. When you draw, you utilize parts of the brain connected with emotional responses and imagination (even if you are not artistic and can draw only stick figures). When emotions and imagination are engaged on a task, you are much more likely to succeed. So if you want to improve your social skills, draw yourself in the middle of a crowd of people, smiling, laughing, and looking entirely at ease.

Picturing success
Sketching the successful outcome you are aiming for on paper, even if in outline only, will help you achieve it.

Gaining Support

When building confidence, you need allies who will encourage and support you. Look for people who can help you achieve your goals, think about the kind of feedback you need, and learn how to deal with people who seem unsupportive.

> **❝**It is not so much our friends' help that helps us as the confident knowledge that they will help us.**❞**
>
> Epicurus

RECRUITING ALLIES

Think about your current relationships. Who, among friends, family members, or colleagues, makes you feel good about yourself? Identify people who can cheer you up when you feel down, people who challenge and inspire you, and those who can coach you when you are finding it difficult to resolve a problem. Is there anyone else you can think of who may be able to help you? You may wish to pair up with a friend who shares your goals. Speak to your chosen allies, describe what you want to achieve, and ask whether they think it is viable. Find out their opinions by asking, "If you were aiming for this goal, would you do it differently?"

◀ Widening your social circle

Build up your network of supportive friends by socializing and establishing relationships with people who are upbeat and positive rather than those who tend to undermine your confidence or sap your energy.

SEEKING FEEDBACK

A supporter's presence can be very helpful in situations where you are trying to build your confidence. Ask a friend if they would be willing to accompany you when your confidence is being tested to give you feedback on your progress. People will usually be flattered to be asked to help. Arrange to discuss the event afterwards, so that you can analyze what went well and pinpoint areas for improvement.

Maintains eye contact while chatting to host

Stays with friend to offer moral support

◄ **Enlisting support**
Take a supportive friend with you to tackle a confidence-building activity, such as attending a party. Their presence will help to reassure you and they will be able to provide valuable insight into your performance after the event.

At a Glance

• Friends are a source of support and comfort as you tackle your confidence goals.

• An honest friend can act as a benchmark for progress and help to ensure that you do not slip back into your old ways.

• Friends who react negatively to your plans for improvement may have their own agendas and are best avoided.

HANDLING NEGATIVITY

While you might expect people – especially those close to you – to be pleased that you are building your confidence, this may not always be the case. Friends or relatives may feel undermined by your resolve to improve, and some might even prefer you to remain reliant on them. If someone reacts negatively or is unwilling to give you any encouragement, the best tactic is to remain optimistic and not to allow them to deflate you. If someone pours scorn on what you are trying to achieve, then you may decide that the best tactic is simply to pursue your goal and avoid them.

Building on Your Existing Confidence

Achievements are a reminder of what is important in life. Acknowledge and build on your past successes, accept that your weaknesses can be strengths, and create a confidence file or "bank" to inspire and motivate you whenever you need a boost.

▲ **Celebrating your achievements**
Many people take the things they do well for granted because they are so familiar with them. Few parents regularly give themselves credit for a job well done, for example. However, creating a happy, stable home life is a notable achievement that should be proudly celebrated.

VALUING YOUR ACHIEVEMENTS

Many people value personal achievements, such as having a good relationship, academic or career-oriented accomplishments, or material successes. But it is important not to overlook the satisfaction that results from handling a problem or change, such as caring for a sick relative or coping well with redundancy. Think what you have done to make you feel proud, after which life has never felt the same again. This will have been a "defining moment", and it represents an important value to you. For example, perhaps life changed after having children or setting up a new enterprise, reflecting the values of parenting or self-determination.

Useful Exercises

▶ List the most significant events in your life to date. These will have involved major changes. Analyze how you coped to give you greater insight into your strengths and achievements.

▶ Discuss your work and non-work projects over the past five years with a friend. He or she may identify achievements you had overlooked.

▶ Compare yourself favourably with peers who have not achieved what you have done.

SEEING WEAKNESSES AS STRENGTHS

People usually find it far easier to identify their weaknesses than their strengths. Indeed, we often live with perceived weaknesses for years without even thinking to question them. Perhaps you still believe that you are "the shy and quiet one", for example. But a quality that is a weakness in one context can be a strength in another: impatience becomes dynamism; laziness becomes a relaxed attitude; stubbornness becomes strength of mind; shyness becomes sensitivity – a great attribute for relating to others and in being creative. List what you see as your weaknesses. Can you think of contexts in which these could act as strengths? Describe these situations and how you would react.

BUILDING A CONFIDENCE BANK

In a notebook, revisit your greatest achievement and answer the following questions:

- What were your thoughts, feelings, and actions leading up to the achievement?
- What did you do that was so effective?
- How did you think, feel, and act afterwards?
- What did you learn about yourself and what strengths did it reveal?
- Can you use these strengths in your current situation?

You might want to include other achievements, too. Look for items that remind you of your achievements, such as congratulatory cards, letters of promotion, or photographs of significant events, and keep them together – along with your notebook – in a safe place. This collection, which can be added to, is your "confidence bank". You can refer to it whenever your reserves of confidence are low and you need a boost.

Finds note praising her efforts from an ex-employer

▲ **Using your confidence bank**
Whenever you feel nervous or you need to "sell" yourself to someone, such as when attending a job interview, refer to your confidence bank to remind you of how well you coped in a similar situation in the past.

Moving Forwards Constructively

Difficult situations and unhappy memories of the past need to be laid to rest if you are to move forwards confidently. Analyze the past and move on from it, leave behind irrelevant beliefs, review your self-image, and learn to accept yourself.

FOCUS POINT

● Sympathize with yourself to show that you care about yourself, but avoid wallowing in self-pity.

Reviewing Bad Experiences

Assess how much of what happened was due to external circumstances

↓

Try to remember exactly what you were thinking at the time

↓

Try to remember how you behaved at the time

↓

Consider the effect of the way in which you thought and acted

↓

Assess how you could think or act differently in future

ANALYZING THE PAST

Think of a difficult situation in the past in which you would like to have felt more confident. Try to identify why you felt insecure and to what extent your thinking or behaviour contributed to any problems. Did you react too slowly, for example, or perhaps you were too impulsive? Consider how the experience stands in relation to the rest of your life and your future plans. Do you remember it as more significant than it is? Analyzing a situation in this way can help you to find positive aspects of a negative experience. Learn your lessons and then move on.

Making changes ▶
Considering past events can be a constructive way of learning. If you know that you have made a mistake, think how you could avoid a similar situation in the future.

Researches facts so he will feel confident making next presentation

At a Glance

- It is possible to learn and to move on from even the unhappiest experiences.

- Unhelpful labels and negative images of ourselves that we acquire while growing up need to be shaken off when they no longer apply.

- People often accept beliefs about themselves and the world without question, yet often these are inaccurate.

REFRAMING YOUR MEMORY

You can use mental exercises to "reshoot" painful memories, rather like a film director choosing to shoot a scene from a new angle and a different character's viewpoint. You can also use reframing to help you to distance yourself from a memory of failure that haunts you. Choose a memory that you would rather be able to forget. Now replay the scene in your head where your feelings and the outcome are very different.

▼ **Forgetting a bad memory**
To shake off a painful memory, replay it inside your head. In order to help distance yourself from it mentally, keep panning back from the scene until it disappears.

| Replay the memory in your mind | → | Imagine the memory becoming more distant | → | See the memory fade into the background |

REVIEWING BELIEFS

Your beliefs can affect your expectations and success. They may be influenced by religion, culture, or class, and may not be proven. They include ideas such as, "You've got to be really pushy to get on in life", or "Those who ask don't get", or "You shouldn't rise above your station in life." The latter belief can make someone feel like an imposter, overlooking the fact that they have earned their position through merit. Decide whether your beliefs are good moral principles by which to live your life, or untrue myths to be disregarded and left behind.

▼ **Examining your attitudes**
Most of our beliefs are shaped during childhood. Think back to conversations around the meal table – were there sensible rules you had to abide by, or positive sayings that now form the basis of your attitude to life?

REVIEWING YOUR SELF-IMAGE

Many people create labels for themselves that are negative and inappropriate. By labelling yourself, for example as "useless at maths" or "clumsy" or "scatty", you may create a self-fulfilling prophecy by behaving in accordance with the label, even if you have outgrown it. An individual who has just made a nerve-wracking speech at a conference, for example, may still believe that he or she is "shy" because it has never occurred to them to challenge that assumption. Indeed, despite this achievement, their belief in their shyness may still cause them to avoid future invitations to speak. Think about some of the labels you commonly use to describe yourself. Are these labels ones you have recently applied, or have you used them for so long that you cannot remember why you first used them? Consider whether they are truly valid, and discard those that no longer apply.

▼ **Changing the way you see yourself**
Giving yourself negative labels will drain you of energy and affect your ability to cope with life's ups and downs. Work on changing the way you look at things and you will feel much better about yourself, even if you cannot change the situation.

FOCUS POINTS

● Avoid trying to be perfect in all areas of your life; you will be putting yourself under pointless pressure.

● Strive to do the best you can in just one or two areas of life that really matter to you.

❝Always be a first-rate version of yourself instead of a second-rate version of somebody else.❞

Judy Garland

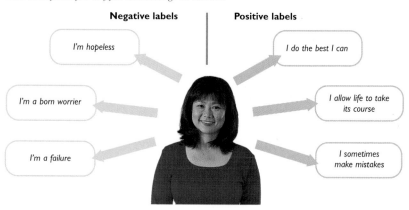

Negative labels

I'm hopeless

I'm a born worrier

I'm a failure

Positive labels

I do the best I can

I allow life to take its course

I sometimes make mistakes

ACCEPTING YOURSELF

Self-acceptance is the process of learning to like yourself "warts and all". No one is perfect, and if you set yourself impossibly high standards you risk disappointment, stress, and decreased confidence. When someone has more talent or skill than you, that does not make them a better person. You have your own unique talents and qualities. Nor is everyone either all good or all bad. Doing something you regret does not make you a bad person, just as doing a good deed does not make someone a saint. Learn to like and appreciate yourself for who you are. This will help you be more tolerant of other people's faults, too.

▲ **Acknowledging imperfections**
If you focus on your imperfections when you look in the mirror, you will only harm your self-esteem. Accept your faults but recognize your good points, too.

Overcoming Negative Styles of Thinking

Style of Thinking	Example	How to Overcome It
Making sweeping statements	"I failed the test; I am a really stupid person."	See a bad experience as situation-specific, not as a reflection on you as a person.
Using extremes to describe yourself	"I forgot my sister's birthday; I am a bad person."	Be more rational and look for the middle route; avoid condemning yourself for one wrongdoing.
Blowing things out of all proportion	"The meeting tomorrow is bound to be a nightmare."	Stop overdramatizing and regain your perspective: what is the worst that can happen?
Belittling your achievements	"That was nothing, anyone could have done it."	Tell yourself that what you have done does count, and give yourself a pat on the back.
Making wild assumptions	"He's yawning – he must think I'm very boring."	Learn to ask people what they really think rather than assume that you know.
Judging yourself against other people	"I should be as articulate as she is."	Accept your own limitations and judge yourself on your own merits.

Projecting Confidence

Projecting confidence involves conveying a sense of being at ease and in control. Learn how to think, look, move, sound, converse, and behave with the utmost confidence.

Thinking Rationally

L earning to think objectively and calmly can help you feel more confident even in testing situations. Learn to focus your attention on other people and what is happening in your surroundings to help you project confidence more effectively.

FOCUS POINT

● In a confrontational situation, try to focus on understanding the other person's viewpoint.

At a Glance

● Self-consciousness disappears when you start to think less about yourself and more about other people.

● In interacting with others, asking questions promotes a more relaxed state of mind.

● A good way to start researching a situation is to look for common ground with other people.

BEING A RESEARCHER

In difficult situations, or those in which you lack confidence, imagine yourself as a researcher who is collating ideas and feedback to improve your understanding of a situation. Good researchers ask constructive questions and review and reflect on their findings so that they are able to handle similar situations more effectively in future. Taking a step back and viewing a situation objectively in this way helps you avoid creating self-fulfilling prophecies when you expect something to go badly. Make sure that your questions are constructive and focused on other people.

FOCUSING OUTWARDS

When you feel insecure, try to avoid worrying what other people are thinking of you. If you are overly conscious of others' opinions, you are more likely to react physically to nerves. Focus your attention outwards so that you are intent upon empathizing and building rapport rather than on how you are feeling. See people and situations as they really are. The more you practise this approach the more you will develop emotional intelligence. Notice how confident people rarely appear to be concerned with themselves at all. They feel secure enough to be able to give all their attention to others.

FOCUS POINT
● If you feel anxiety rising, remind yourself that the feeling will not harm you and will soon pass.

Empathizing with others ▶
In daunting situations, such as business meetings, try to find out more about the people you are talking to and assess their mood to help you focus outwards.

Researching Common Situations

Situation	Questions to Ask Yourself
Meeting someone socially	What does this person do? What is he or she enthusiastic about?
Taking part in a meeting	Who is present? What mood do they seem to be in?
Attending an interview	What does the choice of interviewer say about the employer? How has this employer chosen to conduct the interview?
Making a difficult request	How is the person responding? Should I leave them to think the request over?
Making new friends	What does this person like to talk about? Do we have activities we like in common?

Developing a Confident Expression

An open, friendly facial expression conveys confidence and warmth. By appearing approachable to others, you encourage them to be more receptive to you. Practise making steady eye contact and cultivating a natural, open expression.

MAKING EYE CONTACT

By maintaining eye contact with others, you appear confident because you are showing that you are prepared to engage and communicate with them. Look people in the eye both when speaking and listening so that you are able to note their reactions and respond accordingly. Avoid sustaining eye contact for too long because this can seem aggressive, overpowering, or domineering. On the other hand, too little eye contact suggests nervousness, shiftiness, or embarrassment. Bear in mind that eye contact helps with voice projection, too. If you are speaking to someone yet failing to look at them enough, you will be unable to gauge how loud your voice needs to be.

FOCUS POINTS

● Always look interested and turn to face people when they talk to you, even if you are busy.

● Smile when appropriate, but avoid overdoing it or you risk being seen as insincere.

Registers other person's expression without staring

Uses steady eye contact to show interest while listening

Sustaining eye contact ▶
To maintain the appropriate amount of eye contact, you should aim to meet someone's eyes for between 60 and 70 per cent of the time. More eye contact can make someone uncomfortable, less may make you appear timid.

CONVEYING OPENNESS

An open expression is relaxed and friendly. A winning smile helps, but less expressive personalities may find it difficult to accomplish such a smile naturally on demand, so a slight smile is fine. What is important is to practise relaxing your facial muscles to avoid the frozen or uncomfortable expression that results when you feel nervous and your muscles start to tense.

▼ **Practising facial expressions**
Look in a mirror and assess how the expression that you usually wear would appear to others: does it say "Welcome" or "Go away, I want to be alone"? Try to find ways of looking more approachable.

Self-Talk

Use the following affirmations to help you maintain an open, interested expression when you are talking to someone.

66*I am enjoying engaging with this person.*99

66*I would like this person to feel that I value their opinion.*99

66*I am interested in what this person has to say.*99

Try an expression of mild surprise, keeping the brows slightly arched and opening your eyes a little more widely

Smile with your eyes and mouth – but without showing your teeth

66Laughter is the sun that drives winter from the human face.99

Victor Hugo

Useful Exercises

▶ Relax a tense jaw by dropping your mouth open and yawning while gently stroking down both sides of the jaw with your hands.

▶ Relax your facial muscles by pursing your lips as if you are about to whistle, and chewing lightly, but vigorously.

▶ To create an open expression, relax and drop your tongue behind your bottom teeth. Let the muscles of your mouth form into a slight smile.

Developing Confident Body Language

Confidence is conveyed through body language. Learn how to project confident body signals so that you appear open and comfortable with yourself. By sending out such positive messages you will encourage favourable reactions from others.

UNDERSTANDING BODY LANGUAGE

Signals conveyed through body language are often transmitted unconsciously, which makes them a powerful means of conveying confidence or the lack of it. Barrier gestures, such as crossing the arms or legs, imply defensiveness and a lack of confidence and should be avoided. Confident body language, which can be learned and practised so that it becomes habit, is open and expansive. It involves developing good posture, carrying yourself well, and looking comfortable in your own space. The way in which you walk, sit, and stand, your arm and leg movements, and even smaller hand, finger, or foot gestures provide an insight into your personality and thoughts. You need to ensure that all aspects of your body language are in balance in order to present yourself well.

Analyzing body language ▶
Body positions and movements convey messages about an individual's emotions. Psychologists call this "non-verbal leakage", so it is important to be aware that even seemingly innocuous movements can transmit negative signals.

FOCUS POINTS

● To stand straight without looking stilted, imagine a cord being pulled upwards from the crown of your head and lengthening your neck and back.

● Lean forward a little, if appropriate, to show interest in a conversation.

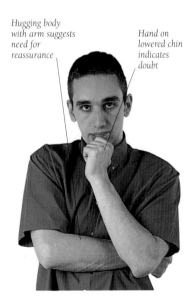

Hugging body with arm suggests need for reassurance

Hand on lowered chin indicates doubt

USING GESTURES

Gestures can be used to enhance your message but should not be allowed to upstage what you are saying. If in doubt, remember that stillness is preferable to movement, especially when you are listening. Keep your hands open when you start to speak because this helps you to appear truthful, whereas wringing the hands, for example, signals that you may not be saying what you think. While you are speaking, you can use open hand gestures to illustrate or add emphasis to your words. Avoid fiddling or touching your face, since these will cast doubt on the authority of your words.

▲ **Looking natural**
Some people use their hands frequently in relaxed conversation, while others are more reticent. Whichever your style, avoid changing it dramatically or you risk looking awkward.

Analyzing Common Postures

Posture	How to Interpret It
Leaning towards someone	Shows enthusiasm and engagement, and suggests an eagerness to build rapport.
Standing asymmetrically	Gives the impression of relaxation and informality.
Standing symmetrically	Suggests nervousness, formality, and stiffness.
Turning away from someone slightly	Implies lack of interest or impatience.
Sitting back in a seat comfortably	Suggests comfort and confidence and a feeling of significance.
Slumping in a seat	Gives the impression of lack of energy, confidence, or commitment, and a lack of involvement.

IMPROVING BODY LANGUAGE

In body language, symmetry conveys formality, so if you know that you stiffen up and become rather formal when nervous, try shifting more of your weight onto one leg. This should help you look and feel less formal. Keep your arms loose and relaxed to give the impression that you have nothing to hide. Lean forwards when standing to show willingness to listen or, if seated, move your body forwards slightly in the chair. Avoid folding your arms and legs and interlocking your hands.

Fact File

According to body language experts, hand gestures not only help to convey meaning to the listener but they also help to coordinate and facilitate the thinking process of the speaker. Research has shown that when people are not allowed to gesture, it can affect their ability to communicate effectively.

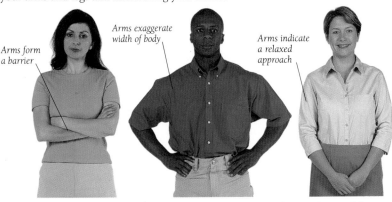

Arms form a barrier

Arms exaggerate width of body

Arms indicate a relaxed approach

▲ **Showing defensiveness**
Arms folded across the body indicate a need for self-protection and suggest lack of confidence.

▲ **Being confrontational**
Putting hands on hips can be seen as aggressive because it represents the assertion of superiority.

▲ **Showing confidence**
A balanced posture, with shoulders back and arms loose, looks comfortable and friendly.

Things to Do	Things to Avoid
✓ Do make a good impression when you are introduced to someone by shaking hands firmly and steadily.	✗ Avoid arriving late at a meeting or social event after everyone else has been introduced.
✓ Do walk with determination and at a good pace but without rushing.	✗ Avoid allowing your face to freeze into one expression or fixed smile – vary your expression to signal attentiveness.
✓ Do pretend that you are hosting an event, even if this is not your official role, to help you greet people enthusiastically.	✗ Avoid fidgeting, for example fiddling nervously with your hair, tie, or pen.

READING SPATIAL SIGNALS

The amount of space an individual appears to occupy speaks volumes about his or her confidence levels. Someone who sits back, relaxes in their chair, and takes up plenty of space seems happy being the focus of attention, and so is perceived as confident. Bear in mind that successful leaders tend to sit and stand higher, whatever their size. Also, space is often associated with status – the larger the office, the more senior its occupant.

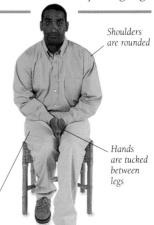

Shoulders are rounded

Hands are tucked between legs

Perched on edge of seat

Showing insecurity ▶
An individual who hunches over and seems to shrink into a seat, taking up a small space, is seen as shying away from attention and so lacking in confidence.

FOCUS POINTS

● Try out confident sitting and standing positions in front of a mirror. Although this will feel artificial, it is a very helpful exercise.

● Get into the habit of checking that you are sitting up straight.

CHECKING YOUR POSTURE

With good posture you can look slimmer and more confident, and improve your breathing. It is easy to fall into bad postural habits, especially if much of your time is spent at a computer screen, but these are simple to rectify. Realign your posture by imagining that a piece of string is holding you up from the top of your head, as if you were a puppet. Relax the back of the neck and shoulders and feel your stomach and back supporting your body, with the spine straight and your bottom neatly tucked under it.

PRACTISING BODY LANGUAGE

Enlist the help of a couple of friends or family members to help you make a video recording. Ask one person to join you in conversation, or help you to rehearse for a forthcoming event. Ask the other helper to record the exercise. Once you have finished, replay the video and ask your helpers for feedback. Keep trying out different behaviour on the video until you are happy that you are projecting confidence.

Using a video camera
If you do not possess – or are unable to borrow – a video camera, you may want to consider hiring one for a day or two.

Looking Confident

Taking an interest in your appearance gives the impression that you are comfortable with your own identity. Even if you have little time to attend to the way you look, you can take a few short cuts to create a confident impression.

GROOMING YOURSELF

Looking well groomed need not involve a great deal of time or money, especially if you cultivate a clean-cut, natural look rather than a contrived one. For women, neutral make-up will flatter rather than dominate. If you do not have time to pay regular visits to a hairdresser, let your stylist know that you would like a low-maintenance cut you can style yourself easily at home. Bear in mind that a hair colour close to your natural colour is more likely to complement your skin tone and also requires less upkeep. Both men and women should invest in regular haircuts and practise good dental and bodily hygiene.

Getting into the grooming habit ▶
Develop a 10-minute grooming routine and do it every morning. Leaving home feeling fresh and presentable gives you confidence to face the day.

FOCUS POINTS

● Look as though you value yourself, and other people will assume that you are capable of valuing them, too.

● A good haircut is a very worthwhile investment, so ask around to find out about reputable salons.

66Appearances are not held to be a clue to the truth. But we seem to have no other.99

Ivy Compton-Burnett

Fact File

Health and beauty treatments have long appealed to women but now men are catching on, too. A growing number are taking a more active interest in their personal appearance and grooming. From a sample of approximately 1,000 men who were surveyed, eight per cent said that they had used saunas, five per cent had used a sunbed, and one per cent had had facials or manicures in the past 12 months. The report predicted that grooming treatments for men were set to become more popular.

Caring for clothes ▶
When buying clothes, bear in mind that natural fibres breathe more easily than synthetics and so may be more comfortable to wear. Get into the habit of putting your clothes on hangers as soon as you take them off, and of leaving them to air overnight before hanging them in a wardrobe.

DRESSING THE PART

What you wear signifies the degree to which you wish to conform and blend in or stand out and express your individuality. Trying to be too different can suggest insecurity rather than confidence. To look confident, you need to feel comfortable, which means wearing garments that fit well, fabrics that hang well, and colours that suit you, whatever your individual style. Choosing outfits that emphasize your good points will make you feel more confident when wearing them.

Clothes that are well cared for look good for longer

REVAMPING YOUR WARDROBE

Set aside at least two days a year as "appearance days", when you give your look an overhaul. Go through your wardrobe and donate any clothes that you have not worn in over a year to charity. Consider whether you need to update your image – it is easy to become stuck in a rut. Look for fashion and grooming ideas in magazines and newspapers, and ask friends and family what they think about your appearance. If people are telling you to throw out your baggy old jumpers, you may need to act on their advice.

At a Glance

● Being well-groomed helps you present a more confident face to the world.

● Clothes that are generously cut can be more flattering.

● Very bright colours are best avoided; if garish lime greens or fuchsia pinks really suit you, consider confining them to accessories such as scarves.

Sounding Confident

When you sound confident, others are more likely to take you seriously. What you have to say will also sound more interesting. Learn some practical techniques to help you control, project, and pitch your voice so that you sound more authoritative.

CONTROLLING YOUR VOICE

In order to sound confident, you need to be able to control your voice. Nerves can cause the tone of your voice to waver and the pitch to rise, and your delivery may sound breathy, or you may gabble. This is because you tend to breathe more quickly in the upper part of the chest, which can also make you sound as though you are gulping for breath. The key to controlling your voice is to slow down your breathing to a more normal rate. If possible, pause to sip a glass of water. Avoid doing battle with your nerves because this will make you more tense. Focus on breathing slowly, and reassure yourself that your nerves will pass.

FOCUS POINTS

● It is easy to become lazy in speech, so make sure that you enunciate clearly.

● Speak at a pace that can be followed easily; people should not have to strain to catch what you say.

▼ **Using breathing exercises**
Practise controlling your breathing and feel the calming effect of taking air deep into your lungs. Imagine that you are inhaling calm and exhaling tension.

At a Glance

● Breathing properly helps you to control your voice and sound more relaxed and in control.

● Improved voice projection can be achieved by focusing on working the speech muscles.

● There is a tendency when nervous to pitch the voice too high, so beware of squeaking.

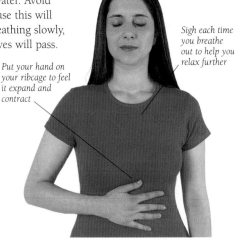

Put your hand on your ribcage to feel it expand and contract

Sigh each time you breathe out to help you relax further

IMPROVING VOICE PROJECTION

If you tend to under-project your voice, you may find it helpful to imagine that your voice needs to occupy more space. Use a simple technique to help you do this: extend your right arm as far as you can, directly in front of your face with the palm of your hand facing your face. Then, while counting to 10, direct and project your voice to your hand. Now, whenever you speak, keep in mind the mental picture of projecting your voice to your extended hand. Another useful technique to help you enunciate more clearly is to imagine that people are having to lip-read you. If your facial expression tightens when you feel nervous, this can make it difficult to project your voice. Slow down, breathe deeply, and exaggerate your mouth and jaw movements just very slightly to get your vocal cords and throat muscles moving more freely again.

Hold the recorder at the same distance from your mouth and practise your volume

▲ **Practising voice projection**
Speak into a tape recorder, giving yourself a volume range of 1–10. Experiment with speaking at different levels so that you learn how each feels and sounds.

Useful Exercises

▶ When your throat feels constricted, just try to yawn a few times (discreetly) to help relax those tight muscles.

▶ If you feel nervous, try sighing gently and quietly to yourself; this will automatically slow down your breathing and your heart rate, and get your voice under control.

▶ When your voice is sounding wobbly, just pause for a beat or two and give yourself a chance to breathe in.

UNDERSTANDING PITCH

Pitch is the note that makes the voice high or low. A low, clear voice conveys confidence, while a high squeaky pitch indicates nervousness. Authoritative speakers, such as newsreaders and politicians, use pitch drops frequently in their delivery in order to convey conviction and gravitas. Your own pitch pattern may be affected by accent but will also be influenced by habit. To sound authoritative, drop your pitch more frequently. On the telephone, holding a pen or using your finger, try pulling the pen or finger down each time you want to sound more definite. Your pitch should drop as you do this, making you sound more resolute. Use the technique to rehearse for demanding situations, such as making a difficult request or public speaking, so that it becomes second nature.

Conversing Confidently

The ability to make good conversation is an essential attribute of confidence. You may already have developed this ability but you can always improve your skills as a conversationalist. Make use of a variety of techniques to develop your talents.

STARTING A CONVERSATION

It can be very daunting to enter a room full of strangers and try to start a conversation. When you find yourself in this situation, take your time to enter and survey the room. Make sure that your expression is relaxed and friendly, and look for someone with whom you might share some common ground. You may notice someone of a similar age to you, or with a similar dress sense, or someone who projects a personal quality that reminds you of yourself. Have some opening questions ready, such as, "Do you mind if I join you?", or, "Do you know many people here?" or, "Have you seen the host?" Show an interest and find out more about someone, such as asking whether they live or work nearby. You may find it helpful to think of a few topics of conversation before the event. Read a newspaper to find a couple of interesting stories that you can talk about.

Using a Framework

> Find out about personal relationships – family, friends, or partner

> Find out about someone's occupation and their leisure activities or hobbies

> Find out about their environment, where they live, how far they are from work

> Keep asking open questions until you find something in common

Chatting with confidence ▶
Try to have one conversation every day with someone you do not know well. A mother, for example, could start chatting to another mother at her child's nursery.

ENCOURAGING CONVERSATION

To be a good conversationalist you need to be a good listener. Active listening skills help you get to know the person you are speaking to and are also crucial in deepening relationships. Make sure that you are listening properly to what is being said and demonstrate this by asking helpful questions when appropriate. These may simply feed back the essence of what has been said, for example, "So you were quite happy about that?" Do disclose something about yourself to encourage the other person to open up. For example, "I know what you mean about driving in town, I'm not keen on it myself".

Leans towards speaker

Enjoys relating story to enthusiastic listener

▲ **Listening actively**
Give your undivided attention to the other person, avoid interrupting them, and use open body language to show that you are receptive and interested in what is being said.

MAKING SMALL TALK

Small talk helps you to decide whether or not you want to pursue a relationship with the person to whom you are speaking. The topic may be superficial but you will be learning about and watching the other person's behaviour in order to discover whether you have mutual interests. Small talk is generally formulaic. One person expresses an opinion or describes an experience and involves the other person by asking a simple question. For example, "Did you come by car – isn't the traffic busy?" Keep conversation flowing by asking open questions, or those that start with words such as What, Where, When, How, and Why, as you try to establish common ground.

FOCUS POINTS

● Remember that most people like to talk about themselves – so ask the right questions to get them to open up.

● To increase rapport, use similar body language to the person to whom you are speaking without mirroring them exactly.

Adopting More Confident Behaviour

One of the best ways to build confidence is to act as though you have it, even when you may not be feeling confident on the inside. Think about how others see you when they first meet you, and take bold steps to change your self-image.

❝We acquire the strength we have overcome.❞

Ralph Waldo Emerson

CHALLENGING YOURSELF

A good way to improve your self-knowledge and practise more confident behaviour is to put yourself in an entirely new situation with people you have never met before. It is often easier to behave more confidently with strangers because they do not have a history with you and so will not expect you to behave in a certain way. You may be surprised at how they respond to you and give you feedback. Consider signing up for an activity that has always interested you such as a gliding or outward-bound course if you like a physical challenge, or joining an evening class to learn a new language.

◀ Being adventurous
Choose a new pursuit that you feel would be really refreshing. Your challenge could be in the form of a demanding leisure activity, such as scuba diving.

SIGNALLING CONFIDENCE

Research shows that first impressions tend to be highly significant. When meeting another person, we immediately look for signs to help us categorize them, and once we have made this initial character assessment it tends to be long-lasting. For this reason, it is very important to make a confident first impression because this is how people will remember you. It is your behaviour – and to a lesser extent the words you use – that will come under most scrutiny. To signal confidence, you need to ensure that your body language and facial expression are in harmony with what you are saying. If there is discord between what someone says and how they say it – such as a guest announcing pleasure to be at a party yet displaying an anxious expression and nervous body language – they will be judged on their behaviour rather than on what they say.

Making an impression ▶
Ask a friend or family member to help you perfect a confident first impression. Make an entrance into a room and greet them with a handshake and an introduction. Then ask for feedback on your performance.

FOCUS POINT

● Believe in yourself and other people will believe in you too.

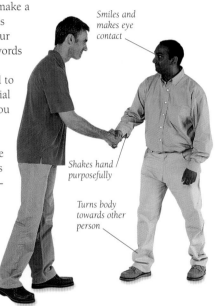

Smiles and makes eye contact

Shakes hand purposefully

Turns body towards other person

Fact File

Body language is far more important than words in terms of first impressions. According to research, we make up our minds about people in the first four minutes based 55 per cent on visual signals, 38 per cent on auditory signals, and only seven per cent on words.

Useful Exercises

▶ Just before you enter a room, tell yourself, "Head up, shoulders down and back, relax the jaw, smile, and breathe out slowly."

▶ Practise shaking hands with a friend to check that your grip is firm but not crushing and purposeful rather than weak or limp.

▶ When meeting other people for the first time, concentrate on how they are feeling and on making them feel relaxed to help keep you calm.

Developing Inner Confidence

We project true confidence when we like and feel at peace with ourselves. Strive to know, accept, and improve yourself by being your own best friend and coach.

Calming Your Mind

*M*editation improves self-awareness and encourages you to take a different perspective on external events and your own personality. Set aside time to refresh your mind, clarify your thoughts, and recharge your confidence levels.

USING MEDITATION

Meditation helps build inner confidence, improving concentration, clarity of thought, and calmness. It stills the active mind and promotes a peaceful, tranquil state that can help to give you greater insight into issues that you wish to explore more deeply. Meditation techniques are simple to master and can be easily practised at home. Set aside about 20 minutes and choose a relatively quiet time of the day for a meditation session – perhaps first thing in the morning, after lunch, or at the end of the working day, to mark a divide between work and your recreation time.

Slows down rate of respiration

▲ **Practising meditation**
Sit in a quiet, warm place where you will not be interrupted. Play background music if this helps you to relax and breathe in and out deeply and slowly. Aim to just "be" rather than try to "do" anything.

RELAXING MIND AND BODY

Feeling calm, in control, and confident is difficult when you are stressed and run-down. Give yourself time to unwind and look after your physical and mental wellbeing in times of duress. Plan at least two "switch-off" periods every day and use these times to unwind, for example by listening to music, reading, watching television, or even gardening if that helps you to relax. Try to take regular exercise, and, when under stress, plan a deep relaxation treatment, such as listening to a relaxation tape or having a sauna or reflexology, at least once a week.

FOCUS POINTS

● Learn to pamper yourself – you probably spoil other people, so why not yourself?

● Limit your intake of stimulants, such as caffeine and alcohol, which can make you feel anxious.

▼ **Benefiting from massage**
Massage alleviates stress and tension that can build up in your soft tissues. It also has a detoxifying effect on the body by getting the circulatory and lymphatic systems moving and so can revitalize as well as relax you.

Therapist applies pressure to loosen tight muscles

IMPROVING CONCENTRATION

To build confidence you need to be able to train your attention to focus on constructive ideas and action, which involves good concentration. To improve concentration, aim to practise on a regular basis. Set aside at least 30 minutes to absorb yourself in a totally involving activity, such as drawing, painting, doing a crossword, or even practising your golf swing. This will help you improve your attention span in the long term.

Enjoying a good book
Reading is an excellent method of improving concentration.

Knowing Your Personality Type

Different personalities are likely to have different needs in terms of building confidence. Find out whether you are more extrovert or introvert to help you identify where you may be lacking in confidence. Then you can work on improving these areas.

ANALYZING PERSONALITY

While most people have both introvert and extrovert personality traits, many people tend towards being one type or the other. To introverts, who have a strong internal focus, clear-thinking is very important. They tend to like structure, order, and clarity – if not in the environment around them, then certainly inside their heads. Extroverts prefer external focus and enjoy interaction with other people. They appreciate endorsement from others, and find people's reactions energizing.

FOCUS POINTS

● Think about your appearance; if you like a simple look that enables you to blend in easily, you are likely to be introvert.

● If you like your look to be attention-grabbing, with detail, print, or pattern, you are likely to be extrovert.

▼ **Recognizing introvert and extrovert tendencies**
Extroverts like to be surrounded by people as often as possible and to discuss their ideas with others, whereas introverts are more introspective and need time alone.

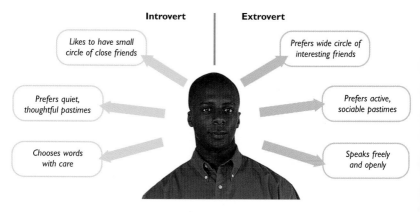

Introvert | **Extrovert**

Likes to have small circle of close friends

Prefers wide circle of interesting friends

Prefers quiet, thoughtful pastimes

Prefers active, sociable pastimes

Chooses words with care

Speaks freely and openly

What Is Your Personality Type?

Read the questions below and tick the box next to the answer you most agree with.

- What do you find most energizing?

a) your own company ☐
b) the company of other people ☐

- How would you best describe yourself?

a) thoughtful and purposeful ☐
b) sociable and outgoing ☐

- What is most important to you?

a) being clear-thinking ☐
b) getting a reaction from others ☐

- What do you most dislike?

a) chaos ☐
b) loneliness ☐

- What do you prefer?

a) achieving things ☐
b) handling other people well ☐

Analysis If you have ticked mostly "a"s, you are likely to lean towards introversion. If you have ticked mostly "b"s, you lean towards extroversion.

Learning to listen ▶
Extroverts often think aloud, which means that they can be tactless. They will benefit from listening more attentively to others, and learning to think before they speak.

BEING MORE EXTROVERT

If you tend to be introvert, you are likely to be confident about your goals and in your way of thinking. You like order, which means planning everything in advance, yet you still worry that you may not be well enough prepared. You may need to be a little less rigid in your thinking. You will benefit from being a little more spontaneous and flexible. For example, going to a large party even though you dislike big gatherings is a good idea – you may even enjoy yourself.

Expressing yourself ▶
Introverts can benefit from practising small talk to encourage them to be more outgoing and feel more confident with new people.

BEING MORE INTROVERT

If you tend to be extrovert, you are likely to feel confident about your outward behaviour and ability to handle social situations. However, the need for constant feedback and reassurance from others is a sure sign that you lack inner confidence. You would benefit from taking some time alone to order your thoughts and think things through a little more clearly. Learning reflective skills, such as meditation and visualization, may be helpful. Socially, you can be a bit of a whirlwind, so slow down a little and think how you can reassure and relax others.

Dealing with Self-Consciousness

Self-consciousness can make you acutely aware of you how you look and sound so that you appear uncomfortable. Forget about what other people are thinking, focus on interacting with them instead, and you will immediately feel more relaxed.

FOCUS POINT

● Use a confident smile as an important communication skill and a simple way of winning others over.

Self-Talk

Use the following affirmations to help you overcome feelings of self-consciousness in social situations.

❝*I am happy in myself – I don't need other people's approval.*❞

❝*I can engage with others simply by listening enthusiastically.*❞

❝*I am going to get to know this person, not worry about what they think of me.*❞

BEING KIND TO YOURSELF

If you become preoccupied with thoughts that other people are judging or criticizing you, you will feel self-conscious and uncomfortable. This happens when your inner critic – the harsh voice in your mind that comments on your performance – gives you negative messages. Perhaps you feel overly concerned with the way you look, or are worrying that everyone else in a group is more intelligent than you. Remind yourself that other people are highly unlikely to be judging you by the same demanding standards you hold for yourself.

Meeting new people ▶
People want to find others engaging, so try not to imagine that other people are criticizing you. Be friendly, show an interest in others, and above all be yourself, and you will feel less self-conscious when meeting new people.

FOCUSING ON OTHERS

Before going into a situation, it is sensible to think about the effect you wish to create. But once you are in a situation, stop thinking about the impression you are making and concentrate on interacting with people, making sure that you pick up on their signals, too. If you feel self-conscious, remind yourself that you should be thinking about how other people are feeling. How would you like them to feel? Involved, reassured, or inspired, for example? Remember, too, that when you give people the feedback they need, you also benefit because they reflect back the feelings they receive from you.

▼ Showing an interest
Self-consciousness can make you appear self-centred, but you can overcome it by forgetting about your own concerns and becoming more interested in how other people are feeling and reacting.

Pleased by interest shown in his work

Takes card and asks questions about business

66Man is the only animal that blushes. Or needs to.99

Mark Twain

THINKING IN THE PRESENT

If you feel self-conscious because you are facing a situation that reminds you of a past embarrassment, keep your mind on the present. If you replay in your mind a mistake you made before, for example stumbling on a staircase, you will feel self-conscious about doing it again. Focus on the here and now by running a mental commentary in your head, such as, "I'm walking down the stairs, I'm keeping my head up, I'm smiling …"

Things to Do	Things to Avoid
✓ Do be genuinely interested in others and think of open questions to ask to help you find out more about them.	✗ Avoid worrying about what other people are thinking about you and just be approachable and natural.
✓ Do aim to reassure other people and make them feel relaxed.	✗ Avoid imagining that others are judging you by your own rigorous standards.
✓ Do keep your mind on the present if you have felt self-conscious in a similar situation in the past.	✗ Avoid replaying in your mind mistakes or embarrassing events that have made you feel self-conscious in the past.

Overcoming Nervousness

Nervousness can undermine confidence, especially when you experience physical symptoms and feel that other people are noticing them. Take steps to control these symptoms and make them less significant, and they will often disappear.

Move shoulders down and back a few times

▲ Releasing tension
Ease nervous tension by stretching your neck and shoulders. Pull yourself up so that your diaphragm has plenty of room to move, then take a few slow, deep breaths to help calm you.

REACTING TO NERVES

The body reacts to stress by adopting one of three responses: fight, flight, or freeze. Most common is flight, which manifests itself in jerkiness, rapid eye movements, nervous fiddling, and quick, breathy speech. In fight response, the reaction is to attack and dominate, resulting in aggression, prolonged eye contact, and sharpness of speech. Freezing, a momentary reaction to stress hormones, may make you feel overwhelmed and unable to speak or move until the panic has passed.

Coping with the Symptoms of Anxiety

Reaction	Solution
Blushing or flushing	Use a green-tinged moisturiser to counteract rosiness.
Sweating	Place your wrists underneath a cold running tap to help cool the entire body.
Stuttering	Slow down, and take a pause to drink water or to take a deep, calming breath.
Shaking	Exercise before important events. To divert tension, clench a small object, such as a pebble, in your pocket.
Nausea	Drink ginger or peppermint herbal teas, or take a few drops of an appropriate flower remedy.

KEEPING A PERSPECTIVE

When you feel nervous, you may lose all sense of perspective about events. The dreaded speech, or exam, or request for a pay rise can loom so large that your other interests in life are quite forgotten. Maintain your sense of perspective by drawing a picture of your life from a bird's eye view, seeing it fully, and in detail. If the dreaded event is in the picture, then put it somewhere small and insignificant. If you are unable to see further than the event you are dreading, take your mind off it and give yourself a reward to look forward to by planning an enjoyable activity for soon afterwards, such as an outing with friends, a shopping expedition, or a sporting fixture.

Self-Talk

Use the following affirmations to put a stop to thoughts that lead to nervousness.

❝Nervousness is not dangerous, it's just uncomfortable. I'm fine.❞

❝When this is over I'll be celebrating because I did it.❞

❝This may seem hard right now but it will become easier.❞

Looking forward ▶
When you are nervous about a future event, think beyond it to a time that you know will be exciting or enjoyable, such as a family holiday. This will help you realize that what you are dreading is, in the scheme of things, relatively insignificant.

SEEING A POSITIVE OUTCOME

Feeling nervous does not mean everything is going to go wrong. Think about whether you are in the habit of predicting disaster scenarios. If you are nervous about taking a test and focus on how awful it would be to fail, you will certainly feel nervous and this will interfere with your actual performance. To reduce nerves, say something positive to yourself such as "I'd like to pass, but the world isn't going to end if I fail". Remember too that a few nerves can be helpful – they can stimulate you to give a better performance.

FOCUS POINTS

● See yourself feeling nervous but still handling a situation you are dreading in an acceptable manner.

● Try a new activity that makes you feel nervous and enjoy the challenge of banishing those nerves.

Using Role Models

Studying the behaviour of confident people and following their lead is a highly effective approach to increasing your own confidence. Choose role models – real or fictional – who inspire you, and imitate their behaviour in situations that test you.

LEARNING FROM OTHERS

Boost your confidence by learning from a role model who has the qualities needed to overcome your own fears. This could be a friend, colleague, film star, or even a cartoon character, or perhaps a composite of two or three people. Observe your role model communicating with others and learn from their behaviour – perhaps they reassure, compliment, involve, or relax other people, for example. Study your role model's appearance and speech to ascertain the type of language they use and the feelings they convey so that you can emulate them effectively.

Changing Your Behaviour

Think of a scenario in which you would like to be more confident

Think of the most confident person you know, living or dead, real or fictional

Visualize your role model dealing with the scenario

Try to emulate your role model's behaviour in real life

Choosing a role model ▶
Your role model should be someone whom you admire, can identify with, and learn from – the kind of confident, positive, happy person that you would like to be.

FOCUS POINT

● If you are unsure what to do, ask yourself what your role model would do in the same situation.

Has successfully overcome obstacles

Has been in a similar situation

Is a good communicator

Inspires your respect

Has a positive outlook

FINDING INSPIRATION

If you are struggling to find an appropriate role model, do some research by looking through newspapers and magazines for interesting interviews. In addition to profiles of well-known people, you will often come across moving stories of ordinary mortals who have triumphed over adversity. You may also find inspiration in the autobiography or biography sections of your local bookshop or by watching television documentaries about the lives of the great and the good.

Learning from life stories
Reading about other people's struggles and successes can prove very inspiring when you are building confidence.

ACTING IN ROLE

When you first adopt the behaviour of your role model, choose a safe, familiar situation in which to "play-act". For example, you could adopt a more confident air with other parents when you take the children to school, or practise parts of a conference speech in routine meetings so it will be second nature when the day arrives. Visualize yourself going through the process of achieving what you want to achieve rather than just producing the end results. See yourself controlling your nerves, practising aloud, and working hard to smile at your audience. Immerse yourself in the character of your role model, much like playing a part in a play.

Practises voice projection during drama class

Useful Exercises

▶ Watch a documentary on a prominent figure who has achieved great things to find out how he or she overcame obstacles.

▶ If your role model is a friend, ask how they built their confidence and if they have any tips that would help you.

▶ Note down phrases your role model uses to make others feel at ease so that you can use them, too.

▲ **Taking centre stage**
Consider improving your acting skills by joining a drama group. Other performance arts, such as singing or playing an instrument, can also build confidence.

Handling Setbacks

Like any self-development process, confidence-building can have setbacks when things do not go quite as planned. Cope with disappointments by retaining a sense of humour, talking about your feelings, and giving yourself a break when necessary.

❝You always pass failure on your way to success.❞

Mickey Rooney

▲ **Making light of setbacks**
Being able to laugh about a setback with a friend, particularly if it has been a humiliating one, will help to make you feel less uncomfortable about it.

KEEPING A SENSE OF HUMOUR

Being able to see the humorous side of a setback or disappointment helps you keep a healthy sense of perspective. Humour is an important part of confidence, because feeling confident means not taking yourself too seriously. It is only those who lack confidence who worry about protecting a fragile self-image. When you make mistakes, try to laugh at yourself and make other people laugh too, to lessen embarrassment all round. Realize that setbacks are probably not very significant when seen in context with the rest of your life. If your life seems to be lacking in humour generally, revive your spirits and enjoy some hilarity by going to see a funny film, play, or comedy show.

TALKING IT THROUGH

If a speech received a cool reception, or you felt shy and uncomfortable at a social event, talk about it afterwards. This will help you cope with the disappointment and see the experience in a different, more positive light. Describing what happened can also help you make sense of what went wrong or identify whether your expectations were unrealistic. By repeating your story to several people, you will also desensitize yourself to any uncomfortable emotions it arouses.

FOCUS POINTS

● Allow yourself a "misery half-hour" after your setback to consciously fret over what happened.

● Once your worry period is over, consign the setback to history.

Useful Exercises

▶ If you are in danger of being discouraged by a setback, constructive visualization can help. Replay the setback in your mind and visualize the final scene disappearing into the background.

▶ To keep you focused on your confidence goal, visualize how you will look and feel as you achieve it, making the scene large and vivid. Savour this image and think of it whenever a setback comes to mind.

TAKING A BREAK

It is important to avoid pushing yourself so hard that you exhaust your resources of energy. Sometimes when something goes wrong, it can be a sign that you are trying too hard. Perhaps you have been focusing so narrowly on your goals that you have lost all sense of perspective. If you suspect that to be the case, it is a good idea to turn your attention to something entirely different. Take time out to relax properly and forget about your confidence-building goals for a while. You can return to them later when you feel revitalized.

Case Study

NAME: Richard
ISSUE: Shyness
OBJECTIVE: To feel more comfortable when talking to strangers

Richard's job involves a lot of business-related socializing. Richard feels fine about talking to people once he knows them, but finds talking to strangers difficult. He goes to a launch, where he knows no one, and tries to make conversation – but no one seems receptive. He goes home demoralized. Richard resolves to tackle this setback, and the next day talks to his boss, who wonders whether Richard was launching himself at people over-enthusiastically. Richard agrees, and starts to see the funny side of it. He decides to forget about the issue entirely for a few weeks, and to play the role of researcher at the next event. He asks for help and information from everyone he meets at this launch and feels that he has become much more confident at socializing with strangers as a result.

◀ **Revisiting a hobby**
Take up a leisure activity, or old hobby, or just relax for a while and see friends. Spend time away from whatever it is you are trying to do and refresh yourself.

Being Your Own Confidence Coach

To build confidence, you need to learn to be your own best coach. Review your progress and goals, give yourself constructive criticism, celebrate successes, and assess longer-term plans to identify areas you may need to work on in future.

Coaching Yourself

Review your goals regularly to check that they are valid and realistic

⬇

Look at what you have achieved and make sure that you have rewarded yourself

⬇

If you have experienced any setbacks, consider how you can learn from them

⬇

Assess whether you are still on target to achieve your long-term goals

⬇

List any actions necessary to help reach your target

CHECKING YOUR PROGRESS

Stay motivated by reviewing your progress on a weekly or monthly basis. Have you achieved what you set out to achieve? Are your long-term goals still clear and vivid? If you have failed to achieve a goal within the time frame given, assess why. Did you fail to plan and organize yourself well enough, for example? Or perhaps you need more support from family and friends? Check that your long-term goals are still realistic and that they reflect your personal priorities and values. Consider whether you are projecting a more confident image – are there areas that still need work?

Making time to reflect ▶
It is important to set aside time for quiet reflection in order to make sense of past events and keep yourself focused and motivated as you make progress in developing confidence.

BEING CONSTRUCTIVE

In order to improve, you need to identify what is working well so that you can do more of it. If, for example, your goal is to speak up in meetings, and last time you made one or two good points, consider why you were successful. Perhaps you were confident because you had done your homework prior to the meeting and were sure of your facts? Learn from this and ensure that you continue to do your research. Think what else you could do to help you speak with more confidence. Could you expand your area of expertise, for example? Avoid negative criticism, since this will demotivate you, and instead look at positive ways of changing and developing your behaviour.

Acknowledge your successes first

Note areas for improvement last

June 26

Julia's dinner party

What went well

Felt surprisingly relaxed. Got on really well with Sarah, who sat next to me. Played researcher role and found we had a lot in common. We arranged to visit an art exhibition together in two weeks' time. Contributed to the general conversation and voiced my opinion a couple of times – didn't stutter or stumble once!

What could be improved

Was a little intimidated by another guest, Charles. I imagined him picking holes in what I was saying. Next time, I will try to think less about what someone is thinking of me and concentrate on making them feel comfortable. I still need to work on my body language – I kept my arms crossed a lot of the time.

▲ **Following a constructive pattern of criticism**
Sit down as soon as possible after a confidence-building activity to assess how it went. Express your feelings candidly so that when you review your account later, you will vividly recall how you felt and be able to see your progress more clearly.

Useful Exercises

▶ Decide how much time you can set aside to reflect on progress – a minimum of four to six hours per month is usually needed if you are taking confidence-building seriously. Choose a less-important activity that you could sacrifice for a couple of months.

▶ In a diary, write the date of your next progress review, book times for reflection, and underline them as appointments that are not to be missed.

▶ Gather together any additional resources, such as inspirational books or tapes, that you will need for this exercise.

At a Glance

● Progress should be reviewed on a regular basis to keep you focused and motivated.

● Constructive criticism will encourage you, negative criticism will discourage you.

● Writing about confidence-building activities helps clarify your thoughts and can prove inspirational later when you re-read your accounts.

CELEBRATING SUCCESSES

Everyone likes to be rewarded for completing something they needed or wanted to do. Giving yourself a pat on the back and praising yourself for a job well done are essential if you are to remain happy and motivated. To make the reward system work, you must choose rewards that you really want. Large or small, expensive or cheap, if it is not something you want, it is not a reward. What is your idea of an affordable luxury? Perhaps you dream of being able to relax with a book for an hour or so or being able to splash out on a good bottle of wine? The size of reward you choose should be commensurate with the amount of work involved. Finally, if you do promise yourself a reward, you must give it to yourself.

FOCUS POINT

● Broadcast your successes but keep any setbacks between yourself and your closest friends.

Rewarding yourself ▶
Knowing that you have a major treat in store when you achieve an important goal will reinforce your motivation. Why not reward yourself by spending a day doing something really adventurous or unusual?

Things to Do

✓ Do plan your rewards in advance so that you are able to budget for them.

✓ Do choose treats that reflect the difficulty of a challenge – you will enjoy a reward all the more if you feel it is well deserved.

✓ Do motivate yourself by putting details of planned rewards in a prominent place.

Things to Avoid

✗ Avoid denying yourself a promised reward because you are too busy or have more important things to do.

✗ Avoid belittling your achievements – every small step represents a success.

✗ Avoid allowing other people to make you feel guilty about spending a little more time on yourself.

MAKING OTHERS FEEL GOOD

Being more confident in yourself makes you more aware of how other people around you are feeling. If you recognize a lack of confidence in someone else, give them your support. Listen to them, encourage them, give them positive feedback, and be generous with genuine compliments. You may even feel able to accompany friends and provide moral support at their confidence-building activities. Helping other people to feel better about themselves will help you feel good about yourself, too.

Showing that you care
Do you know someone who has had their confidence knocked recently? Boost their morale by sending flowers.

LOOKING AT THE LONG TERM

Set a date to give yourself an annual review, perhaps during a holiday, at the start of the year, or on your birthday. Use this as an opportunity to reflect on all areas of your life and make new resolutions where you feel that you could do with more confidence. Record your successes and set yourself new challenges for the year ahead. Remember that you increase confidence by taking control of life and lose it when you sit back and allow things to happen.

List your achievements in the past year

Notes

	Achievements	Future goals
Personal	Quit smoking and feel much better about myself	To make sure that I keep going and stay free
Work	Positive appraisal. Achieved all my targets	Apply for next senior position that becomes available
Social life	Have made a couple of new friends through going to book club	Get back in touch with old university pals, David and Karen
Relationships	Had the confidence to end unhappy relationship at last	Enjoy being single for a while
Health and fitness	Started going to gym	Buy a bicycle so I can cycle to work

Set yourself goals for the year ahead

FOCUS POINT

● Make no more than six resolutions for the year ahead so that you do not feel overwhelmed.

▲ **Conducting an annual review**
Create two columns in your journal, one to list achievements and the other for future actions. Fill in some categories in the first column to start, then move on to the second.

Assessing Your Confidence Levels

Evaluate your confidence levels by responding to the following statements. Mark the answers that are closest to your experience. Be as honest as you can: if your answer is "Never", mark Option 1; if it is "Always", mark Option 4; and so on. Add your scores together, and refer to the analysis to see how confident you are.

Options	
1	Never
2	Occasionally
3	Frequently
4	Always

How Do You Respond?

	1	2	3	4
1 I am happy to start talking to strangers.	☐	☐	☐	☐
2 I love trying out new activities.	☐	☐	☐	☐
3 I have a clear set of goals in my life.	☐	☐	☐	☐
4 I am quite content spending time alone.	☐	☐	☐	☐
5 I can tolerate a fair amount of uncertainty.	☐	☐	☐	☐
6 I feel confident talking to authority figures.	☐	☐	☐	☐
7 I know that I look well-groomed.	☐	☐	☐	☐
8 My body language sends out confident signals.	☐	☐	☐	☐
9 I make confident eye contact with people.	☐	☐	☐	☐

	1	2	3	4
10 My voice always sounds confident.	☐	☐	☐	☐
11 If I feel nervous, I can pinpoint why.	☐	☐	☐	☐
12 I can control any self-conscious feelings.	☐	☐	☐	☐
13 I learn from mistakes I have made in the past.	☐	☐	☐	☐
14 I can hold my own in social situations.	☐	☐	☐	☐
15 I am not afraid of a job interview.	☐	☐	☐	☐
16 I am able to control my facial expression.	☐	☐	☐	☐
17 I know my strengths and weaknesses.	☐	☐	☐	☐
18 I have a clear idea of my priorities in life.	☐	☐	☐	☐

	1	2	3	4
19 I can stop to think when under pressure.	☐	☐	☐	☐
20 I can ask for help when under pressure.	☐	☐	☐	☐
21 I like voicing my views to other people.	☐	☐	☐	☐
22 Public speaking is a challenge I relish.	☐	☐	☐	☐
23 I enjoy starting up a new project.	☐	☐	☐	☐
24 I can focus my whole attention on others.	☐	☐	☐	☐
25 I speak fluently in all situations.	☐	☐	☐	☐

	1	2	3	4
26 I am happy to enter a room full of strangers.	☐	☐	☐	☐
27 I can take the lead in building relationships.	☐	☐	☐	☐
28 I have no qualms about negotiating a pay rise.	☐	☐	☐	☐
29 I feel mentally focused under pressure.	☐	☐	☐	☐
30 I can handle being the centre of attention.	☐	☐	☐	☐
31 If I feel nervous, the symptoms do not last.	☐	☐	☐	☐
32 I feel that I can give confidence to others.	☐	☐	☐	☐

Analysis

When you have added up your scores, look at the analysis below to establish how confident you really are. Then make a note of your weakest and strongest areas of confidence. You need to work on these weak aspects in order to improve.

32–64 Your lack of confidence is holding you back in many areas of your life. Work on building up confidence to help you become more assertive.

65–95 You have high self-esteem, but confidence-building strategies will help you to handle some areas more effectively.

96–128 Your outgoing approach means that you feel at ease in most situations but it is important to avoid complacency.

My weakest points are:

_____

_____

_____

_____

My strongest points are:

_____

_____

_____

Index

LRC Radbrook

Acknowledgments

AUTHOR'S ACKNOWLEDGMENTS

I would like to thank Anthony Jayes and Vicki McIvor
for their contagious tenacity in this project.

PUBLISHER'S ACKNOWLEDGMENTS

Dorling Kindersley would like to thank the following for their help and participation:

Photographers Steve Gorton, Matthew Ward

Models Francesca Agati, Christine Appella, Angela Cameron, Nicolas Chinardet,
Celine Cordwell, Cynthia Gilbert, Barbara Guthrie, Deron James, Ben John, Janey Madlani,
Rosa Mignacca, Camilla Moore, Naomi Nmadu, Sagaren Pillay, Andrew Sheerin, Sheila Tait,
Suki Tan, Peter Taylor, Silvana Vieira, Jeremy Wallis.

Make-up Evelynne Stoikou

Jacket Designer John Dinsdale
Jacket Editor Jane Oliver-Jedrzejak

Indexer Patricia Coward

Picture research Anna Grapes
Picture librarian Sue Hadley

PICTURE CREDITS

Key: *a*=above; *b*=bottom; *c*=centre; *l*=left; *r*=right; *t*=top

Corbis: 6*br*; JFPI Studios, Inc. 28*bl*; Ariel Skelley 33*br*; Steve Prezant 44*br*; Jose Luis Pelaez, Inc. 62*cl*;
corbisstockmarket: Rob Lewine 30*cl*; **Digital Vision Ltd:** 37*cr*, 41*tr*; **Getty Images:** 4, Ryan McVay 56*br*;
Image 100 Ltd: 23*cr*; **PhotoDisc:** 9*cl*, 50*bl*, 59*cr*, 63*bl*, 66*cr*; **Rim Light:** PhotoLink 48*br*;
The Stock Market: Ronnie Kaufman 11*bl*.

Jacket photography © Eyewire and Dorling Kindersley

All other images © Dorling Kindersley
For further information see: www.dkimages.com

AUTHOR'S BIOGRAPHY

Philippa Davies has an MSc in psychology and runs her own business, www.getupandgrow.co.uk.
She specializes in coaching in communication and influencing skills to a wide range of eminent
clients that has included two prime ministers. Philippa wrote and presented the BBC1 TV programme
Tomorrow the World, about building confidence. She is also the author of several books, contributes
to newspapers and magazines, and regularly speaks at conferences on presentation skills and confidence.